W9-CAH-991

Nn Oo Pp
Qq Rr
Ss Tt Uu
Vv Ww
Xx Yy Zz

Copyright © 1980, 1981 by Children's Television Workshop. MUPPET Characters © 1980, 1981 Muppets, Inc. All rights reserved under International and Pan-American Copyright Conventions. ® Sesame Street and the Sesame Street sign are trademarks and service marks of the Children's Television Workshop. Published in the United States by Random House, Inc., New York, and simultaneously in Canada by Random House of Canada Limited, Toronto, in conjunction with the Children's Television Workshop. Distributed by Funk & Wagnalls, Inc., New York, N.Y. Manufactured in the United States of America.   8 9 0   0-394-84946-9

volume **6**

BIG BIRD'S
SESAME STREET
DICTIONARY

FEATURING JIM HENSON'S SESAME STREET MUPPETS

LETTERS O–Q

---

by Linda Hayward

illustrated by Joe Mathieu

Editor in Chief: Sharon Lerner

Art Directors: Grace Clarke and Cathy Goldsmith
with special thanks to Judith M. Leary

Funk & Wagnalls, Inc./Children's Television Workshop

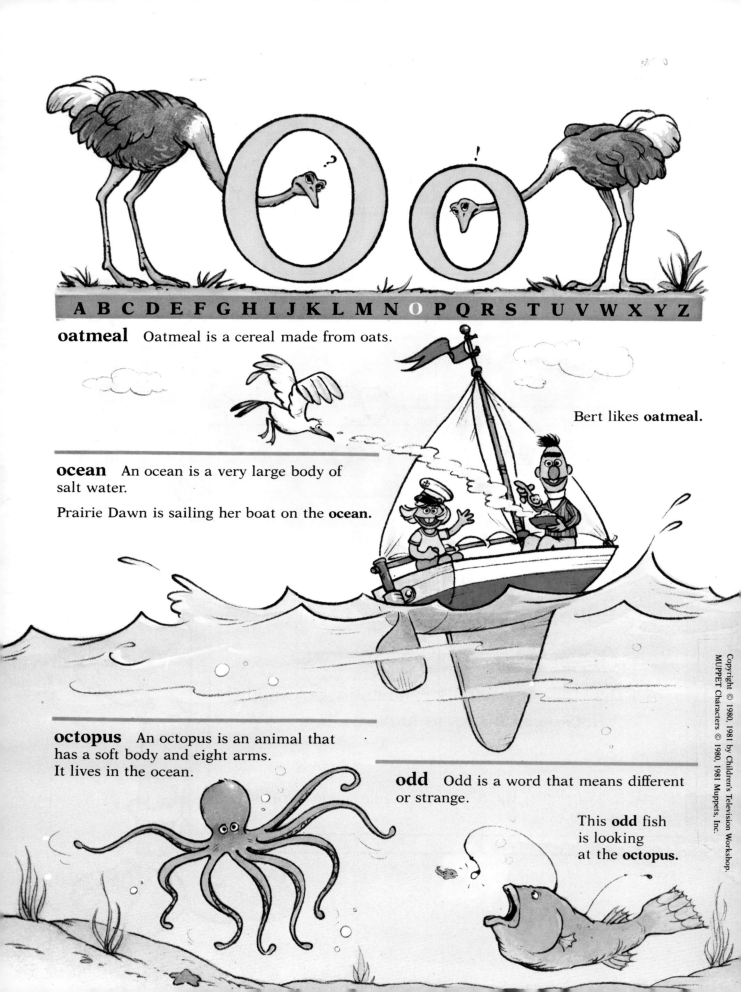

O o

A B C D E F G H I J K L M N O P Q R S T U V W X Y Z

oatmeal   Oatmeal is a cereal made from oats.

Bert likes **oatmeal.**

ocean   An ocean is a very large body of salt water.

Prairie Dawn is sailing her boat on the **ocean.**

octopus   An octopus is an animal that has a soft body and eight arms. It lives in the ocean.

odd   Odd is a word that means different or strange.

This **odd** fish is looking at the **octopus.**

Copyright © 1980, 1981 by Children's Television Workshop. MUPPET Characters © 1980, 1981 Muppets, Inc.

Other Things That Live over or in the Ocean

of   Of means coming from or belonging to.

Half **of** the pie is missing.

office   An office is a place where people work.

Farley's mother is president of the Tick Tock Clock Company. She is working in her **office**.

Mommy, do you know what time it is?

of   Of also means containing or made from.

I have a loaf **of** bread, a jar **of** peanut butter, and a bottle **of** milk for our picnic. What do you have, Ernie?

I have this sign, Bert.

KEEP OFF THE GRASS

PEANUT BUTTER

MILK

off   Off means not on.

off   Off also means not in use.

Ernie, you can turn **off** the radio. The Pigeon News is over.

THE DAILY BORE

often   Often means again and again.

Herry Monster **often** breaks things.

I can't help it.

old   When something is old, it is not new.

How do you like these **old** rags?

Old also means how long someone has lived. I am five years **old.**

on   On means touching or covering.

Marshal Grover is **on** his horse, Fred.

on   On also means not turned off.

Shhh, Ernie. I'm listening to the radio. The Pigeon News is **on.**

once   Once means one time.

Woof!

How many times did Barkley bark?

He barked **once.**

one   One is a number. When you count, you begin with the number one.

1 ... **one** Cookie Monster!

only   Only means by itself or no more than.

There is **only** one Cookie Monster.

Thank goodness! This is my **only** cookie.

open Open means not closed.

The door is **open**.

open When you open something, you uncover, unfold, unlock, or remove a part of it.

Ernie had to **open** his door…so he could **open** his mailbox…so he could **open** his letter.

opposite Two things that are opposite are as different from each other as they can be.

Big is the **opposite** of little.

Little is the **opposite** of big.

We are sitting **opposite** each other.

Opposite also means on the other side of.

or Or means one but not the other.

orange An orange is a round fruit that grows on an orange tree.

Farley, do you want a grapefruit or an **orange**?

I want an **orange.**

Orange is also the name of a color.

Look up the word color.

orchestra   Most orchestras have string, woodwind, brass, and percussion instruments.

cymbals

kettledrums

Percussion

Brass

trombone

tuba

snare drum

piano

French horn

Woodwind

oboe

bassoon

flute

orchestra conductor

trumpet

clarinet

baton

String

cello

sheet music

bass

viola

violin

podium

orchestra conductor   The orchestra conductor is the person who leads the musicians.

The Amazing Mumford is the **orchestra conductor.**

ostrich   The ostrich is the largest bird in the world. It cannot fly but can run very fast.

Hey, Big Bird, the dictionary says that the **ostrich** is the largest bird in the world.

Oh, yeah?

other   Other means not the same as the one being talked about.

There is only one meatball on this plate. I ordered two meatballs. Where is my **other** meatball?

Here is your **other** meatball, sir.

our   Our means belonging to us.

This is **our** bicycle. The bicycle is **ours.**

out When something is out, it is not in.

Betty Lou is in the cannon!

Betty Lou is **out** of the cannon!

outdoors When you are outdoors, you are not in a building.

Bert is indoors.

Ernie is **outdoors.**

outside Outside means not inside.

What are you doing **outside** your nest?

I'm painting the **outside** of my nest today.

oven An oven is a closed space where things can be baked. An oven can be part of a stove.

Cookie the baker bakes bread in an **oven.**

over Over means above.

The Amazing Mumford waves his magic wand **over** his hat.

over Over also means again.

The trick didn't work, Mumphie. Do it **over.**

over Over also means the other side up.

If you don't turn your hat **over**, Mumphie, nothing can come out.

over Over also means finished.

The Amazing Mumford's magic show is **over.**

own When you own something, or something is your own, it belongs to you.

I **own** two broken umbrellas. Aren't they wonderful?

There is only one great O word. Can you guess what it is?

OSCAR

P p

A B C D E F G H I J K L M N O **P** Q R S T U V W X Y Z

package   A package is a bundle or a box with something inside. Sometimes a package is wrapped in paper and taped or tied with string.

Hey, Bert, here's a **package** for you!

Nifty, Ernie! My pigeon T-shirt finally came.

page   A page is a piece of paper in a book, a magazine, or a newspaper.

Everything I've ever wanted to know about pigeons is in this book, Bert.

But, Ernie— the **pages** in that book have nothing on them.

That's right, Bert. That's all I want to know about pigeons— nothing! Hee hee hee.

paint   Paint is used to color or protect things. Paint is wet when you put it on something, and then it dries.

Biff and Sully are using green **paint** on the wall.

pair   A pair is two things that go together.

Bert has a **pair** of gloves, a **pair** of Argyle socks, and a **pair** of saddle shoes on the clothesline.

pajamas   Pajamas are clothes to sleep in.

Prairie Dawn is ready for bed. She is wearing her **pajamas.**

YAWN !

pal A pal is a good friend.

palace A palace is a very large and fancy house.

Prince Charming lives in a **palace.**

pan A pan is a metal or glass dish that is used for cooking.

Cookie Monster is frying an egg in a **pan.**

pants A pair of pants is clothing you wear over your hips and legs.

Bert cannot decide which pair of **pants** to wear.

paper Paper is flat and thin and is used to write and paint on. Paper is also used for wrapping packages and covering walls.

Three of these things belong together. One of these things is not the same.

The **paper** airplane, the news**paper,** and the magazine are made out of **paper.** The frying pan is made out of metal. The frying pan does not belong.

parade A parade is a group of people who are marching together—usually to music.

What is blue and red and purple and green and comes down the street making a lot of noise?

The Monster Day **parade**!

parent   A parent is a mother or a father.

I'm her mother.

I'm her father.

*They are my **parents.***

park   A park is a place outdoors where people can have fun. Sometimes a park has a playground in it.

Bert likes to feed the pigeons in the **park.**

part   When you have a part of something you have some but not all.

I have a whole apple.

*Now I have **part** of an apple.*

YUM!

party   A party is a group of people having fun together.

*Hi, Oscar! I'm on my way to a birthday **party.***

*Ugh! Birthday **parties** are no fun. Why don't you stay for my mud **party**?*

pass   When you pass something, you go by it.

*We **pass** Mr. Hooper's store on our way to school.*

HOOPER'S STORE

paste Paste is something you use to make things stick together.

I am using **paste** to **paste** these pictures into my scrapbook.

pat When you pat something, you touch it gently.

PAT THE DOG PLEASE!

patch A patch is a piece of cloth or other material that is used to cover a tear or a hole.

There is a **patch** on Super Grover's cape.

path A path is a narrow trail that people or animals walk on.

Little Red Riding Hood is walking on the **path** to grandmother's house.

GRANNY'S

pay When you pay for something, you give money for it.

I will **pay** you fifty pennies for sweeping the floor.

Then I will **pay** you fifty pennies for a new bag of marbles.

MARBLES MARBLES

MARBLES 50¢

Help Little Red Riding Hood find the right path to Granny's birthday party.

pea   A pea is a little, round green vegetable. Peas grow in pods on vines.

peach   A peach is a round fruit with fuzzy skin and a pit in the middle. Peaches grow on peach trees.

peanut   A peanut is a vegetable that grows under the ground. The seed inside the shell is good to eat.

pear   A pear is a fruit with smooth skin. Pears grow on pear trees.

Big Bird is picking a **peach.**

I can reach this **peach.**

Farmer Grover grows **peas** on his farm.

I can reach that **pear** if I stand on this ladder.

I can reach this **peanut.**

pebble A pebble is a small stone. A pebble is usually smooth and round.

*This **pebble** will be great for my **pebble** collection.*

peek When you peek at something, you look quickly.

*Get ready! I am going to let you **peek** at Slimey.*

pen A pen is a tool used for writing or drawing with ink.

*I can write my name with a **pen**.*

pencil A pencil is a tool used for writing or drawing. A pencil mark can be erased.

*I can write my name with a **pencil**.*

penny A penny is a coin. A penny is worth one cent. Look up the word coin.

*I have six **pennies**.*

*I have one nickel and one **penny**.*

Each of the Busby twins has six cents.

people Children, women, and men are people.
These are some of the **people** in Big Bird's neighborhood.

Plumber

Carpenter

DOCTOR FRANKLIN

Doctor

GROCERIES

Harry's BARBER SHOP

Barber

Garbage Collector

Grocer

BAKER

Police Officer

Baker

Mail Carrier

Paper Girl

GAZETTE

Cab Driver

TAXI

Fire Fighter

TAXI

F.D.

perfect When something is perfect, it cannot be better.

*I am a machine. I am **perfect.** I do not make mistics... mistocks... mistooks....*

Sam the robot makes mistakes. Sam is not **perfect.**

person A person is a child, a woman, or a man.

*I am a painter. I am the **person** who paints the walls.*

*I am a plumber. I am the **person** who fixes the pipes.*

*I am a window washer. I am the **person** who washes the windows.*

pet A pet is an animal that is loved by the person who takes care of it.

photograph A photograph is a picture taken with a camera. The person who takes the picture is called a photographer.

click!

The **photographer** is taking a **photograph** of Bert and his **pet,** Bernice.

piano A piano is a musical instrument with white and black keys that you press with your fingers.

Don Music is playing the **piano.**

Mary had a little...

...dog?

pick When you pick something, you pull it away with your fingers.

Betty Lou likes to **pick** flowers.

pick Pick also means choose.

*Oscar, I have a nice surprise for you. **Pick** a hand.*

*A nice surprise? Hmmm. Maybe it's a sour pickle or a rotten egg. Okay, I **pick** the right hand.*

Yucch! You call that a nice surprise?

picnic A picnic is a meal that is eaten outdoors.

I brought my favorite food to the Grouch Day **picnic**— sardines with chocolate sauce.

GROUCH DAY PICNIC

picture A picture shows how something looks. A picture can be a photograph, a painting, or a drawing.

This is a **picture** of me when I was a baby.

pie A pie is something to eat. Most pies are round and have a crust on the outside and a filling on the inside.

What does Frazzle Monster like to put in his **pies**?

His teeth!

GRUNT! GRUNT! SLURP!

piece A piece is one part of something.

I want a **piece** of pie.

pig A pig is an animal with four legs, a short nose called a snout, and a curly tail.

Farmer Grover is feeding his **pigs.**

I am a baby **pig.** I am called a **pig**let.

I am the **pig**let's mother. I am a sow.

I am the **pig**let's father. I am a boar.

pigeon A pigeon is a bird with a small head, a chubby body, and short legs.

Bert loves his **pigeon,** Bernice. Bernice loves Bert.

pile A pile is a group of things lying on top of each other.

Here is a **pile** of dirty laundry. I will wash it.

Here is a **pile** of clean laundry. I will fold it.

pillow   A pillow is a bag filled with something soft. You can rest your head on a pillow.

Cookie Monster, do you know what a **pillow** is for?

Sure, Betty Lou. You sleep on a **pillow.**

I thought you were going to say you eat it, Cookie Monster.

!

That good idea! Mmmm … Delicious!

pilot   A pilot is someone who flies an airplane. A pilot is also someone who steers a ship.

I'm an airplane **pilot.**

I'm a **pilot** on a ship.

S.S. SESAME

place   When you know where, you know the place.

My favorite **place** is a pond— with ducks and frogs and lily pads.

My favorite **place** is the dump.

pin   A pin is a short, thin piece of metal used to fasten things together.

This is a straight **pin.**

This is a safety **pin.**

plain   Something that is plain is not fancy or decorated.

Sometimes I like to wear a **plain** hat.

Sometimes I like to wear a fancy hat.

plate 27

plan   When you plan, you decide what you are going to do before you do it.

plant   A plant is any living thing that is not an animal. Trees, flowers, and grass are kinds of plants.

plant   When you plant a seed, you put it in dirt.

Sam the robot is watering the **plants.**

plate   A plate is a flat dish.

play When you play, you do something that is fun.

Big Bird likes to **play** hide-and-seek with Snuffle-upagus.

play When you play a musical instrument, you make music.

Bert likes to **play** his accordion.

play A play is a story that is acted on the stage.

The Sesame Street **Players** are performing a **play.**

Open sesame!

please Please is a friendly word to use when you ask someone to do something for you.

plenty When you have all that you need, you have plenty.

Ernie, would you **please** put oatmeal on the grocery list?

We already have **plenty** of oatmeal, Bert.

plum A plum is a small, round fruit with smooth skin and a pit in the middle. Plums grow on plum trees.

These **plums** are ripe. They look yummy.

plumber A plumber is someone who knows how to fix the water and gas pipes in a building.

The **plumber** came to Farley's house to fix the kitchen sink.

plus Plus means added to.

Two **plus** one is three.

pocket A pocket is a place in your clothes where you can put things.

Prairie Dawn likes to keep her pet lizard in her **pocket.**

poem A poem is a special way of saying something. Many poems rhyme.

Mary had a little lamb. Its fleece was white as snow. And everywhere that Mary went, the lamb was sure to go.

Grover's **P** Poem

I wrote a **pretty poem**
all about the letter **P**
because I know lots of **P** words—
just listen and you'll see.

Pickles, plums, and **popcorn,**
and a **pot** of **purple punch,**
pumpkin pie and **pizza**—
all these **P**'s are good to munch.

Some **P**'s are fun to **play** with,
like **pinwheels** in the **park,**
or **paper planes** and **party** hats,
or **puppy** dogs that bark.

I have a little secret
that I have to tell out loud.
I won first **prize** for **P** words
and oh, I am so **proud**!

point   A point is the sharp end of something.

The witch's hat has a **point**.

point   When something points, it shows the way.

This sign **points** to the cave of Mr. Snuffle-upagus.

TO THE CAVE OF MISTER SNUFFLE-UPAGUS

poison   Poison is something you should not eat or drink because it can make you sick or can kill you.

When I see one of these pictures on something, I know it means **poison**, and I should stay away.

pole   A pole is a long, narrow piece of wood or metal.

Oops!

Grover is painting the flag**pole**.

police officer   A police officer is a person whose job is to make sure people obey laws.

Mr. **Police Officer**, can you tell me how to get to Sesame Street?

Sure. Right after I give you a ticket for not stopping at that red light.

pond   A pond is a small body of water. A pond is bigger than a puddle and smaller than a lake.

Farmer Grover likes to swim in the **pond** with his ducks.

pony   A pony is a small horse.

Prairie Dawn likes to ride her **pony**.

pool A pool is a pond or a special place made for people to swim in.

Betty Lou likes to dive into the swimming **pool.**

poor Poor means not having enough money to buy the things you need.

I always send birdseed to my cousin Bartholomew because he is too **poor** to buy it for himself.

BIRD-SEED

poor Poor also means unlucky or unhappy.

Poor Bert. He is all out of oatmeal.

OAT-MEAL

popcorn Popcorn is a special kind of corn that pops when it is heated.

The Count is popping **popcorn.**

... four hundred and ninety-three ... four hundred and ninety-four ... Oh, I love to count the pops!

porcupine A porcupine is a small animal covered with stiff, sharp hairs called quills.

I wonder why some people say that a **porcupine** is like a big pin cushion.

Oh!

PRESS

possible When something is possible, it can be done.

Is it **possible** that someone brave and smart and strong will hear us calling for help and come to our rescue?

It is **possible.** I can help them.

post office A post office is a place where people can buy stamps, mail letters and packages, and pick up their mail.

Marshal Grover went into the **post office** to mail a letter to his mother.

pot A pot is a deep, round container. Some pots are for cooking and some are for planting flowers in.

Oscar is growing stinkweed in a flower**pot.**

potato A potato is a vegetable that grows in the ground.

Farmer Grover is digging up a **potato** for his dinner.

Farmer Grover is baking the **potato** in the oven.

pour When you pour something, it flows from a container.

power Power is energy or strength to do something.

Pour me another glass of milk, Sam!

It gives me **power** to ride and rope.

practice When you practice, you do something over and over until you can do it better.

Big Bird is learning to use a lasso. He needs to **practice** more.

present A present is something nice you give to someone for a special reason.

Granny Grouch sent me a **present** for my birthday. I hate **presents.**

Hey, great! It's just what I wanted. A banana peel! Granny Grouch always picks the right color, too. Heh, heh.

pretend When you pretend, you make believe or imagine.

Bert, you **pretend** to be Little Bo Peep and I'll be your sheep.

You look silly in that sheep costume, Ernie.

pretty When something is pretty, it is pleasing to look at.

price The price of something is how much it costs.

Pamela Monster is trying on a **pretty** hat.

What is the **price** of this hat?

$45.00

prince A prince is the son of a king and a queen.

princess A princess is the daughter of a king and a queen.

I am the king.

I am the queen.

I am the **princess.**

I am the **prince.**

prize A prize is a reward for winning or doing something.

Cookie the baker won a **prize** for the best cookie.

Your cookie is delicious!

Your **prize** is delicious!

1ST PRIZE COOKIE CONTEST

problem A problem is something that is difficult to do or a question that is hard to answer.

How will I get out of here?

Biff has a **problem.**

promise When you promise to do something, you agree to do it.

I **promise** to take good care of your plants while you are away.

protect When you protect someone, you keep danger away.

Don't worry! I will **protect** you.

proud When you feel proud, you feel good about yourself.

When I help people, I feel **proud.**

pudding Pudding is a soft cooked food. It is usually sweet and is eaten as a dessert.

Mr. Smith wants **pudding** for dessert.

I'll have rice **pudding** …

No, I'll have bread **pudding** …

No, I'll have chocolate **pudding** …

No, I'll have tapioca **pudding** …

puddle A puddle is a small pool of water on the ground.

Big Bird likes to step in **puddles** when he is wearing his boots.

pull When you pull something, you take hold of it and move it toward you.

Farmer Grover is trying to **pull** his mule into the barn.

push When you push something, you make it move away from you.

Betty Lou is trying to **push** Farmer Grover's mule into the barn.

puppet A puppet is a doll that moves when you pull its strings or put it on your hand.

I want you to meet my **puppets,** Crummy and Yucchy.

put When you put a thing somewhere, you place it there.

Mr. Chatterly is going to **put** his chair next to the fireplace.

puzzle A puzzle is a toy with pieces that fit together.

This is my favorite **puzzle.**

puppy A puppy is a young dog.

The **puppy** is following its mother.

It's no picnic being in this dictionary! I have to put up with all those dumb words like party, play, please, present, and pretty. I can't stand it!

The **Princess** and the **P**

A Funny Fairy Tale about the Letter **P**

Once upon a time there was a **princess** named **Penelope.** One day **Penelope** was **picking posies** in the **park** when it began to **pour.** She walked and walked, but she couldn't find the **path** back to her **palace.** And the rain **poured** and **poured. Poor Penelope** was dripping wet and lost.

Suddenly she saw a **pretty palace.** But it was not her **palace.** "I wonder who lives in this **place,**" she thought. So she walked up to the **palace** and **pounded** on the door.

At last the door opened, and standing there was a king and a queen. They were the **parents** of **Prince Paul.**

"Who are you?" they asked.

"I am **Princess Penelope,**" she said.

The king and queen were looking for a **person** who could teach **Prince Paul** how to **play** the **piano.** But only a real **princess** would do.

"Can you **play** the **piano**?" they asked **Penelope.**

"**Perfectly,**" she answered.

Then the king whispered something to the queen, who said, "A real **princess** wouldn't be out in the **pouring** rain. You are just **pretending** to be a **princess.**"

"I **promise** I'm a real **princess**, and I'll do anything to **prove** it," **pleaded Penelope.**

The king and queen began whispering again. Then the queen smiled at **Penelope** and asked her to come in.

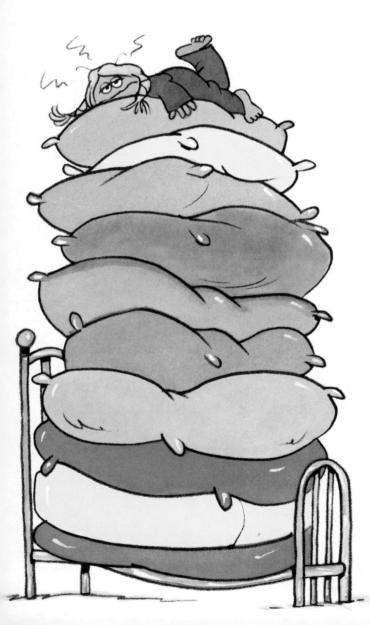

"All right, you can sleep here tonight, but tomorrow you will have to **prove** that you are a **princess**," said the queen.

She gave **Penelope** a **pair** of **Prince Paul**'s **purple pajamas** and went upstairs to **prepare** a bed for the **princess.** The queen put a big **pile** of **pillows** on the bed. Then she **pulled** a tiny **P** out of her **pocket** and **put** it under the **pile** of **pillows.**

"Your bed is ready, **Princess Penelope**," the queen called.

The next morning the king and queen asked **Penelope** how she had slept.

"**Poorly!**" said **Penelope.** "Is it **possible** that you **put** a **P** under my **pillow**?"

The queen rushed to **Penelope** and gave her a big hug. "Oh, **Princess Penelope**," she said, "you *are* a real **princess**!"

The king kissed **Princess Penelope.** "Now, my little **princess**," he said, "you can teach **Prince Paul** how to **play** the **piano**." And he led her to the royal music room.

Prince Paul was sitting in the corner **playing** with his collection of **pigeon** feathers.

"Come, **Prince Paul**," said the king. "We have found a real **princess,** and now she will give you a **piano** lesson."

Prince Paul did not want to **play** the **piano.** He just wanted to **play** with his **pigeon** feathers. But when the **princess** told him to start **playing** the **piano,** he did.

The **princess played** the **piano perfectly,** and soon **Prince Paul** was **playing** almost **perfectly.** The king and queen watched happily.

After **Prince Paul**'s **piano** lesson, the **princess** said, "One thing is **puzzling** me. Why do you need a real **princess** to teach **Prince Paul** how to **play** the **piano?**"

"Because," said the queen, "only a real **princess** can order **Prince Paul** to **practice!**"

So every day **Princess Penelope** came to **Prince Paul**'s **palace,** and every day **Prince Paul practiced playing** the **piano.** Soon he **played perfectly.** And to thank **Princess Penelope,** the king and queen gave her a **pretty purple P** on a necklace, which she wore happily ever after.

Q q

A B C D E F G H I J K L M N O P **Q** R S T U V W X Y Z

quarter A quarter is a coin. A quarter is worth twenty-five cents. Look up the word coin.

Each of the Busby twins has twenty-five cents.

I have a **quarter.**

I have twenty-five pennies.

quarter A quarter is one of four equal parts of something.

Zounds! A **quarter** of the pie is missing!

queen A queen is a woman who rules a country. A queen can also be the wife of a king.

The **queen** is sitting on her throne.

I proclaim today National Be Kind to Grouches Day!

Aaggh!

question A question is what you ask when you want to know something.

Do you have any sardine ice cream with pickles?

The answer to that **question** is no.

quick Quick means fast.

That brown fox is **quick.**

quiet It is quiet when there is no noise.

At last it is **quiet** and I can get some sleep.

?

The Q section went quickly— but not quickly enough. I have just one question.

When are you going to turn the page so I can quit looking at you?

How many things that start with the letter
O, P, or **Q** can you find in the fruit and
vegetable parade?

PIES FOR SALE

QUEEN OF THE PLUMS